Mastering hypnotic language!

Further confessions of a Rogue Hypnotist

By the Rogue Hypnotist

Also available on Amazon in the Rogue Hypnotist series:

'How to hypnotise anyone!' (Amazon.com and Amazon.co.uk no 1 bestseller in hypnosis titles.)

'Powerful hypnosis!' (Highest rating Amazon.com no 3 and Amazon.co.uk no 2 bestseller in hypnosis titles.)

'Wizards of trance!' (Highest rating Amazon.com no 1 and Amazon.co.uk no 1 bestseller in hypnosis titles.)

Disclaimer: the Rogue Hypnotist accepts no legal liability for the use or misuse of the information contained in this book. People who are not qualified professionals use the information at their own risk. This book is intended for entertainment and educational purposes only. Only the hypnosis scripts, deepeners contained within are for your personal or public use copyright free. They may not be resold.

It is a convention of this book to use British English spelling and American English punctuation.

Copyright © 2014 The Rogue Hypnotist

All rights reserved.

CONTENTS

	Acknowledgments	7
1	**Welcome to book 2 in your rapid hypnosis mastery!**	8
2	**The language of hypnosis and trance.**	13
3	**Words beginning with RE are hypnotic.**	21
4	**PMR: (Progressive Muscle Relaxation) and why it works...**	24
5	**Conscious and unconscious dissociation.**	37
6	**Colour feelings.**	40
7	**Hidden code hypnosis.**	43
8	**More hypnotic language: the power of negations.**	46
9	**Reverse speech and the unconscious.**	51
10	**The 'Advanced' hypnotic mind model.**	53
11	**Temporal and spatial predicates: language in time and space.**	62
12	**Utilising utilisation.**	67

13	**Have you ever...**	71
14	**Get to the point: I need specifics!**	73
15	**'Nominalise' this: hypnotic concepts.**	83
16	**Non specified comparatives.**	86
17	**Non specified verbs, people and things.**	92
18	**Hyperbolic words.**	94
19	**Hypnotic poetry: assonance and alliteration.**	96
20	**Some more languaging.**	98
21	**Associational networks.**	108
22	**Ambiguity and confusion.**	110
23	**Adverbs to tell people what to think and feel.**	118
24	**Not now but soon! How to construct 'deepeners.'**	121
25	**Embedded commands hypnotic induction.**	124
26	**Embeds that induce trance.**	131
27	**Describing a state revivifies it.**	136
28	**Your 1st bonus: Symbolic deepeners.**	141

29	**Your new language power!**	149
30	**Appendix 1: PMR script.**	151
31	**Appendix 2: Conscious and Unconscious Dissociation script.**	161
32	**Appendix 3: The Silly Hypnotic Deepener.**	163
33	**Appendix 4: 1st Bonus - The Symbolic Deepener script.**	165
34	**Appendix 5: 2nd Bonus Deepener – The Unicorn Deepener.**	173

ACKNOWLEDGMENTS

*I would like to thank **words**: they can create a prison or the keys to freedom.*

Welcome to book 2 in your rapid hypnosis mastery!

First off folks, if you haven't yet bought book 1: 'How to hypnotise anyone,' I suggest you do. It will give you all the basics for the foundation of your hypnotic success. However this book stands on its own too. It is slightly longer than the first: I'm giving you even more goodies! This second book focuses on more advanced hypnotic techniques and gives you a broader model of the mind with regards to hypnosis: primarily it is about 'hypnotic language.' *Much so-called hypnotic language is of no use to anyone! This book gives you the stuff that works.*

This is, obviously, the second in my series of how to hypnotise anyone books. The first book taught you the basics, if you've read it you'll be 99% ahead of the competition. It gives you a method, a formula, a set of repeatable principles (this is the basis of scientific research by the way) that pretty much allow you to hypnotise everyone. Now we are taking it 'up' a level. I want you to have so much skill with your hypnotic language that you can make it up all by yourself.

All the things I will teach you work. I use them in private practice. If you haven't read my first book let me tell you why you should read this book (apologies if you've read book 1!).

I am a professional clinical hypnotherapist and psychotherapist and an Advanced Master Practitioner of NLP. I know what I am talking about. I have studied this subject for over 20 years now. I have helped crack addicts, depressives, smokers, people who have been left in 'untreatable' agony by incompetent surgeons who have butchered them, armies of weight loss clients, stressed police officers on the brink of a nervous breakdown and more! I am *very* successful with clients. They get what they pay for. They leave with a big smile on their face. It usually takes me one session to help 99.9% of clients.

I'm going to let you in on the 'language patterns' that work as opposed to all the junk out there that will never work in reality. 99% of what is taught on courses is expensive, time-wasting garbage! *Lots of hypnosis teachers are teaching students that if they talk like a weirdo they'll get anything they want in life. If you believe that even I can't help you!* If you talk like a lot of NLP and conversational hypnosis gurus suggest you'll end up sounding like a freak. You need to talk as normally as you can; especially in hypnotherapy, remember: *no one likes mind bending language.* In fact no one wants their mind bent at all! The purpose of 'therapy,' of hypnosis is to help people achieve freedom! Freedom from problems that have tormented them and most importantly: freedom of mind!

I'll teach you how the brain/nervous system processes words. I'll teach you how to be even more 'artfully vague' and how to be very specific. They are two sides of the same coin: one will help you hypnotise others easily, the other will allow you to ask just the right questions to get all the information you need in order to help your clients or unravel potential B-S from many differing sources that seek to influence you covertly.

I'll also teach you how to use even more tricks of the trade: observations, experiences, theories and approaches to hypnotise anyone; which embedded commands actually create trance and hypnosis and how to construct deepeners that work every time. I'll give you

THE 100% fail safe formula for next to nothing. We'll touch on cultural and marketing hypnosis and more advanced knowledge of how all humans are and can be influenced. Including you! This is a more advanced book than book 1 but just as simple to learn. You'll find it easy.

By the end of this book, even if you are not a qualified hypnotherapist you will know more about hypnosis and how the human mind really works than 99% of all doctors, 'therapists,' quacks of any persuasion and other 'mental health care professionals.' And what's more unlike them I am not charging you an arm and a leg to learn things to help others.

Some of my clients have described me as a 'miracle worker.' I am not, I have simply worked out through laborious trial and error what works and what doesn't. Your learning curve is about to be seriously shortened.

Ok that's enough waffling let's get you started: time to learn how to use hypnotic language with complete precision. The training wheels will be coming off a bit more than in book 1 and you will be expected to analyse this stuff without me holding your hand so much. But I have provided some great original scripts that will, I hope, really help you. Again: when you know the principles you won't need me. I don't want you to be dependent on me or anyone else to have hypnotic mastery. A chimp could do this stuff!

The language of hypnosis and trance.

There are innumerable myths about supposed 'language patterns' that that will make someone your 'hypno slave' etc. Fortunately they are a load of old rubbish. However: *hypnosis requires precise language use if you are to become very skilled in its use.* I will start to lay out some specific 'language patterns' that when used as a small part of a large whole will help to add up to your hypno success.

A. **The more the more:** *'The more you relax the more deeply you will go.'*

This is a 'single bind pattern.' That is you are not giving someone a choice. The formula is: the more you do x, the more you do y. There is no real reason why you would, it is a false cause and effect chain but in the 'trance logic' of hypnosis it just seems more plausible. Here are some more examples...

*'The more the **listen to my voice** the more you'll learn what you need to.'*

*'The more you **pay attention to that feeling of relaxation** in your torso, the more you'll be aware as it spreads down your legs.'*

*'The more you **enter this state** the more wonderful you'll feel.'*

B. **The deeper you go the better you feel and the better you feel the deeper you can go:** That is the phrase, very simple, very hypnotic. Feel free to use it during trance induction; it is a favourite of stage hypnotists. Sometimes I'll say,

'And the golden rule of hypnosis is, the deeper you go the more wonderful you'll feel and the more wonderful you feel, the deeper you can go, nooowww...!'

C. **Now....**

Now is a very powerful word in hypnosis. You tag it on the end of sentences following a suggestion and it acts as a simple command for the subconscious to do what you just suggested, now.

'In this relaxed state called trance you will learn all you need to learn, now.'

'You can feel confident in situations that used to bother you, now.'

'You have billions of brain cells that can be

utilised in many ways that will surprise and delight you, now.'

The beauty of using the word now is that it is so conversational, no one knows it's a command it just sounds like part of a sentence and you can use it as a run on to another, I'll show you...

*'Imagine the type of exercise you'd really enjoy, the type that would help you easily and **effortlessly lose weight**, now, there are so many ways of being active, so many ways to **be more active** and won't it be interesting discovering which one you'll enjoy most?'*

You might want to throw in a micro-second pause between the rest of the sentence and now – just a beat will do.

D. **This, that, these, those:** This is a simple but effective one.

'This' and 'these' are *associative* words. 'That' and 'those' are *dissociative* words. Let me show you...

'This feeling will remain with you.'

'These changes will manifest in your life,

automatically, without effort.'

Notice how these two words make it sound like the change is *connected* to you or the listener. Use these when you want a client to *keep* a particular change or when you want them to experience something from their point of view – 'this' and 'these' facilitate subjectivity in trance. Now, the others –

'That old pattern of the past is no longer relevant and doesn't bother you in any way, shape or form.'

'Those former ways of being were right for a younger you but as we mature we find some habits that just no longer suit us and we find better ways instead.'

I have used these two words to dissociate or disconnect the client from the behaviours they want changed. <u>*A good way to become a really good hypnotist is to really start to think about the precise meanings and implications to the words that you use.*</u> 'Those' and 'that' create objectivity of mind or what you might call 'distance.'

D. **All the way down:** One of the best and simplest phrases for deepening trance is to say...

'You can go all the way doooowwwn.'

'Downward' is suggestive of going deeper into hypnosis.

More language tricks. Next it's...

E. **That's right!** You could probably induce a trance just by saying, 'That's right,' whenever anyone manifested 'trance behaviour,' that is the physiological signs of hypnosis and trance. It's a reward for the client following suggestions, an operant conditioning technique: like a verbal pat on the back. When you see a client go deeper into trance use it. If they don't use it, *'That's right, only do what you want to do.'* ***'That's it,'*** is an alternative. It's like saying good boy or good girl to a child. You can also say, ***'Good!' 'Per-fect!' 'Fantastic!'*** *Always* be encouraging throughout a hypnosis session. Examples...

While entering trance someone's face twitches – you say – *'That's right.'*

While entering trance someone lets out a sigh – *'That's right.'*

While entering trance a person's head rolls to one side – *'That's right.'*

Now, when you notice 'the moment of hypnotic surrender,' when they let go into trance fully (see book 1) you definitely say, '*That's right!*'

Simple, powerful.

F. **Each and both of you.**

This odd 'phraselet' means your 'conscious and unconscious selves.' It is mildly disorienting, ambiguous and vague. Perfect for hypnosis in other words. Usage includes...

'Each and both of you can benefit.'

'You can feel confident in all areas of your life, each and both of you, now...'

'Each and both of you can listen and learn, really learn.'

G. **And now:** How much more dramatic could you get!? And now tonight's star is...*'And now!'* grabs your attention: which is inherently

hypnotic.

*'And now as you begin to **enter a state of deep hypnosis**.'*

'And now you will notice many amazing changes upon waking, and don't be too surprised if you feel really good for no particular reason, now...'

H. **In a moment:** <u>this seemingly innocuous phrase is probably THE most important, most hypnotic thing you can say to ANYONE.</u> That's why I saved it for last. So why is it just so hypnotic? Before I tell you let me give you its variants. You nearly always want more than one option, to stave off boredom if nothing else.

'In a few seconds...'

'When I say...'

'Not now but in a moment...'

'Soon...'

'Soon, very soon...'

'In a couple of moments...'

What do they all have in common? Time delay, time lag. <u>*Because nothing is wanted of the*</u>

*person **right now** the analytical guard is down.* There is no immediate perception of a threat. It also primes the subconscious to *prepare* to respond when you give the cue. I learnt this by studying top stage hypnotists; before they do any sketch or elicit hypnotic phenomena like hands glued together they set it up with this phrase one way or another. It's perfect to begin deepeners with. We'll get to that in a bit. Ok, that's enough of that for now.

Words beginning with RE are hypnotic.

I have no idea why! Sorry. RE is an instruction to do something that you've done before.

Let me show you with the word:

Re-lax – word origin Latin.

Old French - RE = back to original place; again, anew, once more. *A sense of undoing.*

Lax = soften, loosen (originally referring to digestion hence – laxatives!)

RE Latin derivation = again, back, anew, against.

This is why *hypnotherapy is re-associative*, (more on this in book 3 'Powerful Hypnosis,') a command to relax in effect says – go back to before you were tense. Hints of age regression in that simple word?

Some examples follow…

Realise…you know more than you know, you know…

Recognise…your potential to move past those worries that used to bother you…

Revivify…a pleasant feeling, now…
(Revivification is easy with hypnosis – feelings, resources, memories – you name it.)

Reconnect to…your ability to relax deeply, very deeply…

Resource….after resource is already available to you inside…

Re-associate…to good moods, times and places you felt good…

Re-organise…already existing subconscious structures.

Research…research is looking for something that has already been found. If research were involved in originality it would be called 'search.'

Remember…probably one of the most hypnotic words available. If you say,

'Remember a happy time,'

the listener, reader is instantly thrown into a light trance just to remember one. <u>*Remember when you want to hypnotise someone you turn their attention inward.*</u> See my first book, 'How to hypnotise anyone,' for a full explanation of this principle.

Interestingly a **_re-volution_** is going back to something that already was. The so-called 'sexual revolution' is a good one: it actually means going back to the pre Christian sexual attitudes – thus: neo-pagan sexuality. Oh words, such misunderstood things! A revolution is in fact a return to a past 'Golden Age.' Beginning to see how little of 'English' and its real roots we are taught at school?

PMR: (Progressive Muscle Relaxation) and why it works.

Lots of NLPers and hypnotists poo-poo poor old PMR, that is 'Progressive Muscle Relaxation.' This is the technique whereby just getting a client to focus on the body, specifically the major muscle groups and then suggesting that those same muscles relax deeply produces a very deep and profound state of hypnosis. It can often send someone into real sleep especially if they are really tired or stressed! That's fine. They'll probably grunt themselves awake at some point.

Yes there are other ways to get someone into trance but avoiding a technique for some arbitrary reason is plain stupid. It reminds me of my old English teacher who would never let us use the word 'got.' He had got some kind of 'got fixation.' Apparently he considered it bad English. Often with modern English the Latin words are regarded as 'proper' and the Old Saxon words, the short and to the point ones are regarded as crude and uncouth. This was a product of the Norman Conquest of the English. The Normans spoke Old French and Old Norse, although their origins go back to Finland.

I had another teacher, an art teacher who regarded black as not being a colour (good grief!) and so he wouldn't let us use the black paint and we had to mix it from a special formula that only he knew. So if you wanted to paint a seagull, which is grey and you couldn't remember the secret formula you were f...fed up! It's the same with PMR: it is a technique that works! So why not use it?

<u>Remember one of the golden rules of the mind is: where the mind leads the body follows and where the body leads the mind follows.</u> When you physically relax the body with just your words – you might call it a 'mind massage' the mind calms down too.

As a hypnotist/hypnotherapist you will be meeting people who are incredibly tense and NEED to know how to relax: they have forgotten how to relax. They are so habitually tense that they think the tension is relaxation! PMR will also calm down emotional arousal which is essential so that clients can see beyond their old 'black and white' (actually 'locked in' fight or flight) stressed brain thinking. For example a depressed brain is a stressed brain. Below is a script for inducing hypnosis PMR style. If you haven't read book 1 – use a command/downward inflexion on the embedded commands which are highlighted. I've spiced the script up a bit for you...

PMR script.

'Ok just close your eyes...

and just pay attention to your breathing...

in and out... (time this on the in and out breath – thereby 'pacing' the client's reality.)

That's right...

You don't have to change your breathing at all...

just notice it...

Draw all of your attention to your breathing...

*as you **relax deeply**...*

Now,

just focus your attention on the top of your head...

your scalp...

*Imagine you simply **relax***

all the muscles in the top of your head...

relax *your forehead...*

calming*...yourself...****down****...*

all the way down...

Good...

And now...

your eyes...

your temples...

relaxing*...*

Your ears can relax...

the back of your head too,

supported by that pillow/cushion...

so comfortable...

*Again **relax all** the tiny **muscles***

around your eyelids...

All of them

*can just **let go,***

***relax and unwind**, now...*

The muscles between your eyebrows

can soften,

smooth out...

*take a **rest.***

And even the nose can relax,

tension can accumulate around the nose

but it can melt away now too...

and who knows, (phonetic ambiguity: nose/knows.)

how the nose

knows how to relax?

But it does...

*And female rabbits are known as **does/doze**...* (confusion: non sequitur – 'doze' = command - sleep!)

And you can

effortlessly...

allow this feeling of

pure relaxation

to spread down your neck...

That's right...

so wonderfully relaxed,

peace increasing...

inside...your mind...

because...

as **your body relaxes,**

your mind relaxes...

does it not?

Time to just **slow**...**things**...**down**... (Anxiety is associated with speed. Suggest the opposite. 'Down' also suggestive of going down into hypnosis.)

down to your shoulders...

Just let those shoulders...

relax comfortably.

Don't have to do anything...

for a while...

The back muscles,

releasing past tension.

That old...

tension just melts away...

so pleasant...

that calming, soothing, restful sensation

spreading...

all the way down

your lower back

*increasing **serenity**,* (single word command)

relaxing,

smoothing out certain things...

almost as though,

someone you love deeply

is massaging

all that old tightness you had away.

Your chest and tummy muscles...

feeling so soft,

so wonderful.

That feeling can spread

to where it needs to go.

Just getting rid of any

unnecessary tension,

in the past...now.

And down to your

waste/waist area, (phonetic ambiguity)

feeling

***tranquility, now**...*

And what's the most wonderful thing

about kindness and love?

For yourself too? (Whispered)

Letting those big thigh muscles

relax so pleasantly,

that chair comfortably supporting...

your hamstrings muscles too.

Your arms can relax:

the deltoids,

biceps,

triceps,

the forearms...

all the way down

to your hands,

your palms relaxing...

each finger and thumb...

so comfort-able...

Aware of the feeling

of your interlaced/touching fingers,

the feeling of your jeans...(whatever they are wearing)

any textures...

the different feelings,

in both hands.

One hand might feel slightly lighter,

and the other slighter warmer... (truism – this is often the case.)

And I don't know which hand is the right hand

and which one is left? (Phonetic ambiguity/double meaning for left and right.)

Perhaps...

your calves can

relax next...

your shins,

your Achilles' tendons...

down to your ankles,

top of your feet,

aware of the feeling of the shoes/socks etc. (if they are wearing any) *on those feet...*

your toes too...

each toe relaxing,

one...

by...

one... (suggestive of counting down)

and your sole/soul... (phonetic ambiguity suggestive of 'deep rooted' relaxation)

deeply relaxed.

Your entire mind and body

deeply relaxed, now.

Now I just want for a moment...

to speak to...

you're unconscious (ambiguity – your/you're)

I'd like to thank that part...

that was and is protecting you...

looking out for you...

that was making you

too worried,

stressed,

overly tense…

back then.

But now I would like,

the sympathetic part of the nervous system;

that's the part that takes care

of the arousal phase of the 'fight or flight' response

*to **calm down, now**…*

to allow the parasympathetic phase,

of the nervous system;

*that is the **calming down** phase…*

*to begin to predominate, **now**…*

Only responding to real danger,

when needed.

The old overly tense and stressed pattern,

is unnecessary, now...

That's right.'

You can continue with therapeutic suggestion or just begin an awakening process. Up to you. *<u>Remember most people want and need relief from stress and tension: PMR can help.</u>*

Conscious and unconscious dissociation.

In order you get hypnosis you can use the following technique: the aim? To get the conscious mind and the unconscious to dissociate. You do this by talking about what consciousness does and what the unconscious does. It is done very vaguely as you'll see. Whether hypnosis is just dissociation is another matter, I don't think it is. I use this method as a deepener once I've already gotten someone in a nice light hypnotic state.

Conscious and Unconscious dissociation script.

'As a part of you listens another part becomes more and more immersed in this process...

Maybe one part wants to follow what is happening, while another in fact knows without effort and simply absorbs things...

Perhaps a part may be concentrated on some ideas yet at the same time another can continue on its journey into the inner world of experiences...

A part can doubt and question and another can accept positive change and experience is possible, can understand with more and more trust...

Maybe some part wants to observe and be alert whereas another uncovers its own creative potentials and deeply desires to try something new...

One part may try to exert too much control over everything with its learnt bias, while another deeper part of you is free to imagine some things you desire and put into practise...

A part is preoccupied by the moment as another simply finds it easy to go down stream and act on certain things that please it most...'

Remember you can learn this by heart if you want but working off of scripts is fine: it doesn't make you a 'scripnotist' whatever that means. Dr. Milton Erickson did it sometimes and he invented modern hypnotherapy single-handedly. I think that spending hours of your lifetime learning hypnosis scripts is a TOTALLY unproductive waste of time. I have a life; I am not a hypno-nerd or hypno-obsessive. You learn through repetition anyway not memorisation. The way you learn a script is through muscle memory, that is the muscles of the mouth, tongue etc. (the organs of articulation) 'remember.'

As I hope you noticed all comments to 'consciousness' occurred first – the left hand side of the text and the unconscious was addressed on the right hand side. Incidentally these mirror the hemispheres of the brain which supposedly predominate for each part, left being logical and right intuitive. The hemispheres of the brain are actually much more complicated and the brain/nervous system is a giant interactive neural network. People with physical brain damage have started using parts of the left or right side of the brain to carry out the task of the former hemisphere which was impaired: no one knows anything! Although 'Neuroscience' claims it is mapping the brain I think the human brain is like an internal cosmos: too vast and grand for the puny human conscious mind to ever fully understand. Thank goodness!

Colour feelings.

What the heck are 'colour feelings' I hear you ask?! Simple: the human brain associates/encodes feelings with colours. Why? Who knows? Red usually with anger, passion. We hear it in clichés: 'He was red with anger!' Blue for coolness, calmness, depression/sadness: 'I felt blue.' She was green with envy: it's all in our language fabric. Jealousy: ...'tis the green eyed monster that doth mock the meat it feeds upon.' Depressed people often refer to the depression they feel as 'The black cloud,' Winston Churchill referred to it as his, 'Black dog.' Boys like blue, girls like pink. *The colour yellow makes people more suggestible.* Blues and greens tend to be soothing. Reds, oranges tend to be associated with aggressive, energetic feelings. Now how is this of any use to a hypnotist?

During an induction, quite near the beginning, instead of progressively relaxing the muscles I ask someone to,

'Imagine a colour that makes you feel very relaxed...now allow that feeling, that colour feeling (ambiguous/confusing) *to spread from*

the top of your head all the way down to the tips of your toes.'

You can see this in my basic hypnotic script in 'How to hypnotise anyone,' my first book. I am explaining it thoroughly now. When you understand the theory you will be able to find other applications. It can be used to reduce injury pain, control IBS (Irritable Bowel) gut pain, elicit emotions and cause a woman to orgasm.

A woman once told me she felt anxious in social situations, which people call being 'shy.' I asked her *where* the fear was located. She looked confused (she wasn't used to thinking that way – her attention became focused); she pointed to her solar plexus (feelings are often said to emanate from this point, who knows why??!) I then asked *what colour* is the fear (again confused look); she said red. I asked what would the opposite feeling be. She said blue. In hypnosis I told her to,

'Imagine that (that - dissociative) *red feeling in the solar plexus changing to blue, this* (this- associative) *blue feeling, these* (these - associative) *feelings of calmness and wonderful*

*confidence, now. And they can spread all through your mind and body, making you **feel wonderful, now...**'*

It was of course only part of what I did to help her. I asked afterwards how the solar plexus area felt, had that old feeling gone? She said it had and she felt much better. Aren't we weird?! The way the brain, nervous system *actually* works seems bizarre because it is the opposite of what we are told. No one knows nothing - as Shakespeare once wrote.

I once had a man who said he felt empty and hollow in the solar plexus area as a result of his cruel, abusive upbringing: I used colour feelings in this case too.

You can take any feeling, turn it into a colour and spread it through someone's body: confidence and happiness are two good states to play with.

Hidden code hypnosis.

What I call 'hidden code hypnosis' is really a way of bypassing consciousness and directing a therapeutic suggestion to the subconscious/unconscious. I do this by hiding it, like a hidden code within a larger sentence. I break the suggestion up and disperse it one word at a time in between a piece of writing/speech. Let me show you. Note: in order for hidden code hypnosis to work you must make subtle use of pauses and embedded command tonality – that is a falling tone.

Notice I am actually delivering two suggestions: a longer overt one and a shorter 'covert' one. *Multiple communications which the subconscious can easily process.*

'***You** have many abilities of which you have been consciously unaware...and you **can** discover them because the other mind knows more than you know, you know, so you can really **stop** and find out that the ability to be **using** your natural capacity to feel good without **drugs**, free and healthy, even – in control, all right, **now**. Recognise this hidden truth at some level haven't you? **For** many* *things can change and **your** behaviour can change appropriately so that you **own** these changes and it's the **unconscious** or subconscious that secretly does all the work for you for its own **reasons** without the other knowing or needing to know.'*

The hidden hypnotic code is (obviously): **'You can stop using drugs now for your own unconscious reasons.'** By the way that on its own 'un-coded' would work.

Aha! But there is also a third message to the unconscious! Did you spot it? It is about half way through, the sentence: <u>*'Recognise this hidden truth at some level haven't you?'*</u> The hidden truth being – the hidden hypnotic code.

<u>*If*</u> I use this I add it in quite early in a session after a basic induction and one deepener. You can encode any message:

You feel confident.

You have self-belief.

Scratch your nose.

Do something different.

You can also use this technique in normal conversation without any hypnosis, the unconscious will still pick up the message and it will act upon it quite frequently.

More hypnotic language: the power of negations.

The prime purpose of negation is to attract resistance and so diffuse it. Negations are sneaky ways of delivering suggestions that don't seem like suggestions. Some good examples follow...the first is probably the best, derived from Dr. Milton Erickson's work. It implies choice.

A. You don't have to...

*'You don't have to **relax**.'*

'You don't have to pay any attention to what I'm saying.'

*'You don't have to **feel growing comfort**.'*

*'You don't have to **go into trance** until you want to.'*

B. Don't...

This brings me to the: 'Don't think of pink elephants principle!' *In order to NOT think of pink elephants you have to think of pink elephants.*

'Don't relax too deeply…yet.'

'Don't make any changes you don't want to.'

'Don't **relax your breathing**…'

'Don't notice where you feel most peaceful…'

C. Never. (A don't variant.)

'Never imagine pleasant scenes.'

'Never feel very good until you're ready.'

'Never fall into a deep hypnotic sleep till you know it's what you want to do.'

These sorts of language patterns can be used well with so-called 'polarity responders' or contrarians if you prefer. Certain people like to be contradictory, it's in their nature, perhaps they are natural rebels who knows but if you want to get children like that to do something you can say things like,

'I bet you could never eat all your dinner up.'

They will guzzle it all while looking at you thinking, 'I'll show you!'

D. It's not necessary…

'It's not necessary to try to remember consciously…' (The implication? Forget!)

'It's not necessary to learn consciously…' (Implication? Learn unconsciously!)

*'It's really not necessary to **stop smoking today**…only when **you're ready, now**…'*

Note: much suggestion work can be done through implication. Normal conversations use implication often. All the hypnotic patterns in this book occur naturally but you are becoming aware of them so that you can use them to help people. I will cover implication in detail thoroughly in book 3.

Negations can inoculate against resistance because they don't seem to be suggesting anything. The client has no need to resist; you already did it for them. If that makes sense? <u>Remember your attitude should be, I don't want any power and authority over anyone anyway</u>, when you think like that people don't resist. They see you as an ally, which you are.

E. You shouldn't…couldn't…wouldn't.

'You shouldn't go inside and remember a happy time, but you could…'

'You couldn't make just the right shifts unconsciously until you were ready anyway.'

*'You wouldn't want to **become deeply hypnotised** without becoming aware of your most comfortable big toe.'*

F. Tag questions.

*'You already know how to **relax deeply**, do you not?*

When you tag a question on the end you hide the command/suggestion.

'All these changes have occurred without your conscious mind knowing how, haven't you?'
(The past predicate '…haven't' is non-grammatical and so, confusing and it is a suggestion – '…haven't you?' suggests change has already occurred.)

For God's sake don't be a total twerp and talk like this in real life – you'll sound weird or pretentious or both!

'You've learnt some new habits and you will, will you not? Will you not?'

Again we create confusion but this time with a future temporal predicate 'will' which doubly suggests the new habit will be acted on...you just aren't stating it explicitly. As the client doesn't consciously know what the hell you are on about he won't resist.

'It's easy to learn hypnosis, is it not?'

Notice the hidden command – It is easy to learn hypnosis – the tag question on the end hides it. A bit like an embedded command.

To learn the patterns in this book you might want to write down five examples of your own to train your brain to use this type of hypno-speak. Writing things down helps clarify thought. The trick with all this stuff is that it adds variety to your repertoire. You have a bigger tool box to draw from. Don't overdo these things in practise use them subtly, deftly. *<u>When you think of hypnotic language think precision. Know your intent and use your new languaging skills to achieve it.</u>*

Reverse speech and the unconscious.

As a hypnotist it is a good idea to learn as much as you can about the nature of the subconscious mind and what it is capable of: what its true nature is. In the last few years I have learnt something quite startling about this part of our selves. When we speak we communicate with others in forward speech. Subconscious slips ('Freudian slips'), ideomotor signals may give away the truth of what we really think BUT we also reveal ourselves through 'backward speech.' What do I mean? Record someone speaking. Play it backwards – reverse it and listen out for what the subconscious is revealing in reverse. It takes skill to be able to identify real 'reverse speech' from things that sound as if they might be actual subconscious communications. It is most illuminating to do so with the speech of politicians and people of that ilk. You might be surprised as to how the reverse speech reveals something totally contradictory to what the forward speech claims. Be careful doing this with friends and relatives – you might discover something it's best not knowing! Don't violate loved ones' privacy. No hypnosis teachers will teach you about this stuff. The weird and whacky world of the subconscious! So let's continue in this vein.

The 'Advanced' hypnotic mind model.

In order to build a body of knowledge you must seek truth. If you let conscious sets and biases (social programing) get in the way of this, you will be a much less effective hypnotist/hypnotherapist than you could be. Remember the truth may wholly contradict what you thought was true.

A bit of speculation on my part follows.

Note: all layers can be programmed with unhelpful, unrealistic beliefs.

The Conscious Mind: Predominantly analytical part, programmed with 'conscious sets' - biases and beliefs. Powerful ability to focus, potentially clever but not necessarily wise, potentially deeply analytical: looks out for others' attempts to influence you in ways that could be harmful to you. Academic training focuses at accessing this level. The intellect is but the tip of an iceberg of giant proportions. Intellect is not the same as intelligence. This part consciously plans things and checks that the strategies employed work. Only likes to focus/concentrate on one thing at a time –

otherwise it gets stressed/overloaded, especially men's conscious minds. Women can pay attention to multiple things. This is biological – men focus intently in the hunt, women need a multiple focus to protect a group of children. That said both sexes prefer to deal with one thing at a time.

The subconscious layers protect consciousness. The deeper layers will only 'let through' to consciousness that which they think the surface level can handle safely. The conscious self also represents the social mask, the persona that we want others to see. Affected by logic language unless you are a woman. The so-called 'left brain.' Like a precocious child who thinks he knows it all. The good thing about it is that is very curious and eager to learn.

One of the functions of consciousness is to justify on-going behaviour: that is to make excuses, to 'rationalise.' *If you hypnotise someone to get angry at someone else for no good reason, just because the hypnotist suggested it and the hypnotised person is asked why they are angry, they will justify their anger!* Even though it wasn't their idea. This has huge ramifications regarding whether our thoughts are our own! Think about it.

One of the prime functions of consciousness is to 'think critically,' this faculty is strongly present from early childhood; however is can be crushed if what children experience is repeatedly contradicted by parents, teachers and other 'authority figures.' Why? The child's need for approval and attention, support and survival override the intelligence and function of the critical faculty and the child instead begins to 'parrot' those who have power over it in order to 'fit in' and be a 'good boy/girl.' Totalitarian political cults have always known this and used it to their advantage.

If this form of anti-reality conditioning continues unabated, over time the child develops a 'pseudo self' - the real self, still present yet unconscious remains unfulfilled and unrealised. An example being - doing a job to please parents against one's own deeply held desire to do something else entirely etc. In many ways this must lead in a great many people to a form of mild 'multiple personality'; so the conscious self, presented to the world may not be the real self at all but rather a pale shadow of what it could have been. The conscious self is also forced into various 'roles' and subgroupings of behaviours that are present only in specific scenarios. Once these roles: student, employee etc. are habituated they will become unconscious and so seem normal, and again constitute a mild 'multiple personality.' This of course doesn't mean anyone should be naively, even dangerously honest!

Note1: _All deeper levels are benevolent. The following levels only want to help a person; they never intentionally cause an individual harm. Remember: Freud was a sick, crazy b%$£*^d!_

Note2: _All layers from now on require a different language to communicate with; they are 'non-logical,' 'non-linear': they have their own 'logic'. Speaking logically to them is like speaking English to a French person. Although there are similarities they just ain't gonna understand you._

The Preconscious Mind: a threshold just below consciousness, home of tip of the tongue phenomena. The place where things go just before entering consciousness, perhaps a final checking stop. The 'Google' of mind; the conscious seeks info (memories etc.) and the preconscious 'google' searches for it, placing filters on access to information: the filters are beliefs – the ideas/things people 'believe' to be true. Neuroscience has revealed that people's brain's think thoughts before consciousness knows about them – so they are? Preconscious!

The Subconscious Mind: probably deals with everyday habits, learnt skills that have become automatic (driving, painting, public speaking etc.) everyday emotions and bodily functions. Runs many if not all mind-body systems automatically – digestion, sweating etc. Fight or flight response most probably here – actually the muscle priming response. Most hypnotic change *probably* occurs here. *Deeply affected by emotive language and vague trance/hypnotic language.* Affected by poetry. Like a vast factory or untiring workhorse – remember those cartoons with little men in lab coats running the brain/body – keeps you alive. Many people have suggested that the subconscious is another word for the body. There is probably much truth in this. 'Parts' in part's work therapy are probably located here. This will be explored more fully in book 3. Unlike consciousness, the subconscious can do many things at once – so-called 'multi-tasking.' Dreadful word combo.

The Unconscious Mind: the almost deepest levels of the psyche. Affected by symbols and in charge of dreaming. Discharges all anxiety and emotional rumination that accumulates during the day: this keeps you sane. _Symbols can dramatically program the human psyche and de-condition it too – with regards to the latter only as long as the symbols are subjectively generated._ Powerfully affects conscious behaviour in ways not fully known. Contains unconscious beliefs and awareness that may well be in conflict with conscious beliefs. Deep levels of healing occur here: probably in sleep – the home of the 'placebo response.' Can be programmed through song/music so that certain behaviours manifest as a result. The deeper levels of the mind know more about a person than consciousness does. They can process multiple tasks at once. _Capable of solving problems without conscious help._ Source of all creativity, insights and ideas, the location of all 'instinctive templates' that seek expression, satisfaction in real life. Source of wisdom. A vast ocean of possibilities and potentials lurks here. Perhaps as yet untapped?

The 'Superconscious' Mind: I have added this term in here as a possible alternative to subconscious and unconscious. _It suggests a part that is aware of a great deal more than consciousness – it is 'hyper aware.'_ This is, perhaps, the place of reverse speech which has been touched on. Although consciousness lies (lies are a protective **and** deceptive mechanism) the deeper layers know the truth and always seem to want to express it even by 'sideways' methods. Think about it this way: your brain is bombarded by billions of bits of data – it processes vast amounts of information moment to moment. So it is aware of more than consciousness knows. That is why you can induce trance through overload and redirection of attention to things normally outside awareness in the normal waking state.

The Core: the ultimate core of who you truly are: the place beyond your name; it contains your true sense of self, your deep identity. It knows everything you do and really think and why you _really_ do it. It seems some hypnotherapists call this the 'Hidden Observer,' 'The Wiser You/Self.') This part is split in

MPD/DID (Multiple Personality disorder/Dissociative Identity Disorder,) through horrendous abuse. If you want to talk to deeper structures say something like

'I'm now talking to the deepest part of who you truly are.'

The Soul.

There may be a deeper level still that religions call 'the soul.' The nature of spirit is far beyond the confines of this book and the knowledge of this writer.

In reality most of these parts do not actually exist, they are simplistic names for a complex symphony of processes. The brain is it seems much like an orchestra composed of many parts with their own functions. Instead of going **down**, my model goes **inward** to the core. Like onion layers.

Some hypnotherapists believe that the subconscious can't tell the difference between reality and something imagined. Not true. It seems it may be the amygdala that can't tell the difference, although that too may be just a theory. You can always tell the amygdala to calm down. And just in case that part isn't involved you can say,

*'Can the **part that was overreacting** in that way it was **calm down** (?).'*

*When consciousness gets out of rapport with the deeper layers problems **will** ensue. No ifs or buts!* Clients have been ignoring signals from deeper levels or they wouldn't be your clients. Unfulfilled needs are not being met and unhealthy habits have gotten out of hand. A simple example is a weight loss client who ignores the signal that they are full and carries on eating. *Ignore subconscious signals at your peril.*

Note: *in hypnosis we 'feed' the conscious to the sub-conscious minds.* Temporarily.

Temporal and spatial predicates: language in time and space.

When creating suggestions make sure you use space-time precisely. What do I mean? Hopefully the word use is obvious!

'***Before*** *you relax deeply I just want to say...'*

'***After*** *this session you'll awaken with all changes made, feeling fantastic with the knowledge that this is so...'*

*'That **old** problem you **once had**, in the **past**...'*

*'Imagine a **future** you in a certain situation behaving confidently...'*

*'That smoking behaviour you **used** to do is no longer true about you in any way shape or form...'*

*'That problem that you **had** no longer bothers you...'*

*'You haven't got the change you want **yet.'***

'***Up until now*** *you have been eating portions that were too big...'*

*'When you can see **beyond** this problem imagine all the ways your life has improved...'*

Temporary is a good word ('temp' = time) suggests things won't last. Like problems. **Passing** is another goody.

*'That problem was just a **temporary** companion, wasn't it?'*

*'All suffering **passes**...'*

<u>Words ending in 'd.'</u>

Many words that end in **'d'** put things (problems) in the past. They are suggestive that the desired change has already happened.

*'You don't have to do those things you once **did.**'*

*'You have **changed** in all the ways you wanted.'*

*'You have **learned** a great many things, have you not?'*

<u>So linguistically put your client's problems in the past – their brain will follow suit.</u> Make sure they can see progress in the future, with your

words. They should be able to visualise a problem free future – also known as mental rehearsal. I often say something like,

*'That problem **no longer** bothers you in any way, shape or form, and this is so,'*

as a summation.

<u>And spatial predicates...</u>

*'Now you have put that problem **behind** you...'*

*'You have moved **forward** from where you were temporarily...'*

'Bad' (unwanted) things behind, good things ahead – linguistically. These are just a few examples that can help. Think of your own.

<u>Up and down...</u>

'Deeper...'

*'All the way **down...**'*

'Falling into the wonderful oblivion of trance...'

<u>We induce trance through the language of downward movement</u>*...We wake **up** remember...*BUT you can also intensify feelings

and experience in hypnosis by suggesting someone go **'higher.'** *You can intensify experience in trance by making the imagined reality seem vividly real – like virtual reality.* You can say,

*'I want you to imagine that what is happening is vividly lifelike and real and the **higher** you go into this hypnotic state, the **higher** your most pleasurable feelings will increase...'*

(This is really a variation of the more the more pattern.)

*'The **higher** you go the more your awareness, your sensations, your feelings, the vividness of your experience only increases and expands.'*

This is not the same as so-called 'Hyperempiria' which doesn't exist. In the next book: how to construct a 'heightener!'

Remember when happy we say we felt **high**, good moods go **UP**! 'He is going **up** in the world!' I suggest you could use **'higher'** suggestions to heighten good feelings. I occasionally use it with misery guts and junkies. *All humans are born with all the natural uppers and downers they need.* No external aids required.

Living the **high** life…**high** on the hog…**highlight**…on the **up**! Geddit?

And finally…

In working with internal images that bother a client by causing anxiety you can say,

*'Take that image that **bothered** you, drain the colour out, make it black and white, **push it away into the distance** till it disappears completely…'*

As you can see both temporal and spatial predicates are involved. NLP greatly exaggerates the usefulness of so-called sub modality work. Again this will be discussed in a later book.

Utilising utilisation.

In hypnosis 'utilisation' means using whatever the client or environment offers you, you turn to your advantage: it is a reframe. Whatever someone offers you is to be used or effortlessly transformed.

It seems whenever I get hypnosis clients my next door neighbours bring out a chainsaw to cut their hedge or are turning their nicer gardens into sterile driveways (because it's fashionable!) This involves equipment that sounds like a plane taking off. Could be a teenager drives by playing loud music. Do not despair!

Don't fight, don't panic: use it, whatever it is, however seemingly improbable it is that anyone could be relaxed/hypnotised because of it – trust me, they can. Babies can sleep anywhere, no matter what the noise. People can concentrate on anything fascinating even if the environment is busy (I originally wrote busty!) or noisy.

A client comes in. You start hypnosis and they start giggling! So you say,

'That's great: it is a bit funny isn't it? Me speaking in a funny hypno-voice; but the more you laugh, the more you relax, laughing makes you relax, laughter is an unconscious response...etc.'

Accept their response and use it. Just today a woman said she was excited and wanted to laugh, I simply said,

'Yeah that's normal, it is funny, I'll be putting on a funny voice in a minute, it is silly, the whole situation is ridiculous when you think about it.'

Not a titter.

You are hypnotising someone, your stupid neighbour starts cutting their lawn with a whining lawnmower or a great big fleet of tanker lorries/trucks drives by outside so that the earth shakes! So you say,

'And as that lorry drives by, as it goes off into the distance you go deeper and deeper, that's right...'

'No sounds bother you in any way, shape or form; they just take you deeper...'

If a client awakes to answer a mobile phone or

get comfy, just say,

'That's right just make yourself more comfy/sure answer the phone...'

When they finish (they'll apologise...) you say...

'Not to worry, close your eyes and know that when you awaken from trance it's easier to go deeper than before...all the way down.'

In this example you are using 'fractionation' - the idea that putting someone under and waking them up and putting them under and waking them up takes them deeper (I'll show you how in another book though it is entirely surplus to requirements). It does and here you are utilising the fact that the twit left their phone on (and they will trust me!). They have done you a favour! *Things won't always go to plan, that's life: stay calm and just think: how can I use this?* How can I turn this cockup to my advantage? This is a good use of reframing. What if everything they do only made it easier to hypnotise them? That's a good belief to operate from and 99% of the time it's true.

If someone, it will be a man, tries to resist say,

'That's right you are so powerful, like a superhero, imagine yourself as your favourite superhero fighting against a villain, imagine all the amazing powers you'd have! Perhaps you are flying through the sky!'

As soon as they start visualising, you got 'em.

Have you ever…

Although I have given you lots: I want you to get your money's worth, the simple fact is: *you don't need to use ANY 'language pattern' to get trance or hypnosis.* But 'have you ever' is a good one. How do you use it? Well, firstly what does it do? It really says 'remember or re-access an experience, resource, emotion etc…'

'Have you ever relaxed on a beach?'

This seemingly innocent remark actually asks the brain to do this: find a memory of sitting on a beach in a relaxed state of mind and body. By accessing a relaxing memory the person will access a bit of the relaxation. *The memory and emotions are associated.*

'Have you ever felt confident?'

Everyone feels confident *some* of the time, in certain situations. Even people with phobias are troubled by varying degrees of phobic response. But where am I sending them? To access confidence. I am directionalising the brain. I am starting the re-associative process.
Hypnotherapy re-associates the brain to helpful resources that hitherto the client couldn't

access in a certain situation in a waking state. More on this in my next book.

'Have you ever been in love?'

Ask a woman this and unless she is severely emotionally repressed she will re-access that feeling of love instantly. Be careful using this, not really therapeutically appropriate unless there is some real purpose to asking it.

That's an easy one to remember. Next!

Get to the point: I need specifics!

In order to cut the B-S you need people to be specific. Specific language is the opposite of hypnotic language. It wakes you up and connects to real things instead of abstracts and generalisations that literally do hypnotise people. This has been known far longer than the development of NLP, which often claims to have reinvented the wheel.

'I eat healthily...' says a weight loss client.

'Really what do you eat? Can you outline your daily meals for me?'

'I eat cakes, biscuits blah, blah...'

That honestly happens. Clients and people in general like to lie, fib a bit, give half-truths – it's actually a way of not facing up to reality, rarely it's ignorance. It's your job to – gently, wisely – get the specifics in order to help people. You also need to get specific if an authority figure like a politician is speaking. They are all well trained in neuro-linguistics and psycho-linguistics as are their speechwriters and PR people. You can tell when people like politicians, CEOs, celebrities are lying or dissembling when they are being vague. Honesty is never vague: it is blunt, spontaneous, often brutal like a child. Deception is slow paced – the person is thinking of what to say, how it will be received, choosing words very carefully. If in doubt ask:

'What do you mean by that specifically?

Remember: specifics are grounded in reality. Vagueness is the airy-fairy language of hypnosis. Some examples follow...left hand side is vague statement, right is the question asking for detail. Highlights identify where vagueness lurks.

*'I don't like **that food**.'* '**Which** food?' – Food *type* unspecified.

*'I smoke **too** much.'* 'How **many** do you smoke?' – Actual quantity unspecified.

*'I **lack** confidence.'* 'When/in what situations do you lack confidence exactly?' – Triggers for nerves unclear.

You need detail, detail, detail. Especially when doing hypnotherapy; these interview questions will help you narrow down what you must target to effect change during hypnotherapy.

Words to get specifics...

Clarify, specify/specifically, exactly, precisely.

*'Can you **clarify** x?'*

*'What **specifically** happened?'*

*'What did she say **exactly**?'*

*'**Precisely** what age were you when you first took cocaine?'*

Be careful with asking for specifics: some people want their privacy, respect that and DO NOT interrogate! Unless you desire to be friendless. Try...

Softening openers...

Can I ask...?

May I ask..?

I'm a bit unsure can you explain...?

Oh by the way, clients will often say,

'I bet you think I'm

crazy/weird/abnormal/disgusting?'

or words to that effect. Just reassure them that they are not, their problem is normal and common. They often seek that reassurance. *Problems are normal responses to stress and unmet needs – they are just bad long term responses.* Don't say,

'I've never heard that before! You *are* bloody weird!'

I once had a woman tell me that she saw a psychic who told her she had 'terrible problems' because she was murderer in a past life. I looked at her, paused and said in a funny tone,

'...O-K...'

This made her laugh and we moved on.

When searching for specifics you are doing it because? Something is left out. You cannot complete the picture without supplying your experience to fill the gaps. In other words – the client/speaker has hypnotised you! How do you know what *you* imagine they meant is what they meant? You don't. Again be careful with this – never invasive. Interestingly I heard of a man who got a girl to dump her boyfriend using the NLP Meta Model: the pattern whereby you learn to ask for specifics. Obviously her boyfriend wasn't so great on close inspection! You are gathering just the right info and no more to help someone. Don't be nosey! People have a right and need to privacy and vagueness. I once asked a woman if anything but cigarettes helped her relax. She went into trance and clearly imagined having sex with her ex-boyfriend. After having enjoyed this (her facial expression dummy!) she replied –

'Um...no...' I knew she was fibbing.

'That girl is so pretty!' **'Which one?'** - Person unspecified.

'That took ages to do!' **'What did?'** - Verb/Action – unspecified.

'I saw that film ages ago!' **'When exactly?'** - Time unspecified.

'He's a total d%k!'* **'Why is he a d*%k precisely?'** - Reason unspecified.

<u>*However never ask clients to justify what they think and feel to you. Again:*</u>

when asking for specifics you are looking for what is missing. Your friends to gather info are:

Who? - The person is missing.

What? - The object, animal, action, quality etc. is missing.

Why? - The reasons are missing. (NLP teaches people to *never* ask 'why' questions of clients. This is so stupid as to not even warrant a response; sometimes *why* is exactly what needs to be asked. Like all 'rules' in this field you are better off breaking them. They are like bizarre little doctrines to limit your ability to help others. Just don't ask things like: 'And why do you take drugs when they are so bad for you?' You may privately judge your clients but professionally never! You can still focus on solutions and ask why.)

Which? - The object, animal, action, quality etc. is missing.

When? - The time/duration is missing.

Where? - The location is missing.

How? - The mechanics, the skillset, the strategy is missing.

A question of status.

These are just examples. We all do these things from time to time anyway in normal life.
Remember the person asking questions is usually in a position of a higher social status.
Think of the Queen of England on her rounds,

'And who are you?'

A policeman asks,

'Where were you on the night of the 25th?'

A doctor,

'Where does it hurt exactly?'

<u>You can assume complete control over a brief interaction by asking tons of questions. You are demanding information.</u> I once did this to an annoying sales person on the phone. Again: don't expect to make friends that way though, friendship follows a share and ask pattern. You reveal, I reveal. An authority figure asks and reveals nothing usually. *Have you noticed how we feel compelled to answer questions? You don't have to. There is no rule to say you must. However we are conditioned from early childhood to feel an inner urge to answer. Sales*

people use this against you.

Some clients do ask me personal questions and I nearly always answer them. It makes them feel more comfortable around you, humanises the situation too. I seek to work equal to equal.

There is always a point in an interview when I work out exactly what I need to do to help a client. Many hypnotists do away with this part. I find it vital. How can you help someone you know nothing about? – It's all so impersonal. You use the information gathering stage to work out who your client is and how to help them. The unique person in front of you. Hypnosis sessions must never be generic, although no doubt people with similar problems will require similar interventions. The interview stage is when you get rapport naturally with a client/hypnotee. You get to show your personality to them so that, as one of my clients said, 'I get a good vibe from you.' This also produces the expectation that the therapy will work. Expectation is your ally. *Therapy is not fast food.* I'll go through my standard questions I ask clients in full detail in book 3: 'Powerful Hypnosis!'

Assumptions in trance.

Let's talk about presuppositions. Again an awareness of presuppositions far predated NLP. *What is a presupposition? Anything that is assumed, anything that is pre-supposed, taken for granted as being so.* Let's take the innocuous sentence...

'I am writing this book.'

What does this statement assume?

1. That there is an ***individual*** (me!).
2. That he is ***writing.***
3. And that he is writing a ***book***. Let's try another.

So we assume someone/something is doing something (verb/action) for some purpose.

'The cat sat on the rat.'

So we assume a cat, a rat and that the cat sat on the rat. Now, how do we make use of this in trance?

'Everyone goes into trance sooner or later.'

*'Eventually we all rest and **drift into a daydream,** do we not?'*

What is presupposed? That you **will** go into trance! Not **if** but **when**. Both are truisms: see book 1 'How to hypnotise anyone,' to understand truisms fully.

'How soon will your trance deepen?'

We assume that trance already exists and can only deepen.

'How much deeper into trance can you really go?'

Assumption: you're already in trance but how deep can you *really* go? It suggests you don't yet know how deep you can go, in other words you can go a whole lot deeper Mister! It also assumes discovery: *discovery is hypnotic!* As is curiosity.

'And where will that feeling of comfort spread to next?'

Assumes comfort already exists, to whatever degree (they have to feel a *degree* of comfort right? Even in the big toe, who knows!?); *comfort is a sign of trance,* and that it will spread. It's just a more precise way of using words. Words are your tools to achieve objectives. People with a wider vocabulary have a richer mental life, can think and communicate clearly and can experience reality with more depth. Don't believe me?

'The sky is blue.'

'The sky was a soft Septembral blue. The cool autumn clouds caressed its surface like people sleeping on lilos (US: air matress).'

Now that's too flowery for ordinary speech and a bit pretentious but how much more involved do you feel? Hypnotists should have some knowledge of word history. The word 'confidence' comes from Latin: the prefix – 'con' (meaning 'with emphasis') , version of 'com' and 'fidere' (meaning faith) – so confidence literally means 'having faith in oneself.' _Think about the meaning of words._ Know that the meaning of words changes over time. Those who have never befriended the dictionary before may need to do so. A 100 year old dictionary may seem a foreign language – original definitions are deliberately altered. Read amply: fiction and non-fiction. Have a wide range of interests. You must become an interesting person. By the way a good therapist will have a grasp of current affairs, history and approaching trends; if you don't you will be a-historical, out of touch and unable to understand why people are coming to see you in the first place. Drug addiction was not a 'pandemic' fifty years ago: you need to know why it is now.

By the way good therapists need a full, rich life outside of work. Again: if you want, write out a few examples of these language patterns to train your noggin (brain) how to do it. It's easy I promise: once you start practising the subconscious will start to do it all automatically so you won't even have to think about it. You'll start being vague or specific unconsciously: you won't even know you're doing it half the time. *Just being aware of presuppositions will protect you from manipulation.* News readers (anchors) use them constantly to mould public opinion. Ask yourself: what is being assumed? Is that assumption *evidentially* based? Am I being led to perceive things a certain way? Who benefits from me or you assuming this interpretation of events is true? And who losses out?

Remember that silly saying:

'Never assume anything; it makes an ass out of u and me.'

A few more hypnotic assumptions...

'Will your right or left hand feel heavy or light?'

Presupposes a hand will feel something. Also a double bind (either or choice).

*'Before you **go into trance** and make some amazing changes I'd like you to get comfy...'*

This obviously assumes you will go into a trance! 'Before you' is similar to the 'in a moment' pattern; it primes expectations.

'Nominalise' this: hypnotic concepts.

NLP bases its linguistics theories on Chomsky's work. Chomsky's work has been thoroughly disproven but reification also known as nominalisation predated him anyway. What is nominalisation? Taking a verb (action) or adjective (descriptive word) and turning it into an abstract, (static) noun. For example...

'Relax,' (verb) becomes relaxation (a concept)

Something concrete is turned into an abstraction. If it's not a thing it's a nominalisation...Which itself is a nominalisation – the verb – to nominalise – abstracted/turned into a concept.

Adding a 'tion' from Latin 'sion' on the end of a word does this.

'Aggression,' concept form. Reality - 'He hit me in the face!'

'Religion,' concept form. A very brief word for a whole host of things - ritual, prayer, fasting! Concepts help us be brief.

'Indoctrination,' is the nominalised form of - 'to indoctrinate.'

'Digestion,' - to digest food, ideas.

'Suggestion,' - to suggest something.

'Information,'- to inform. What information?

Note: nominalisations are very hypnotic. Concepts are vague, not agreed upon; they are open to interpretation, that's the point: take...

'Democracy.'

Now that means a lot of different things depending on who you ask.

'Hypnosis' and 'trance' are both nominalisations for highly complex processes. As is 'sleep,' a short word for something so very complex. Sleep is the best nerve tonic ever! Make sure your clients sleep is good, if not fix it.

'Knowing,' 'understandings,' 'learnings' – good hypnotic words.

'Relationships,' 'experiences,' and 'processes,' are very hypnotic too, as is 'awareness's.' Sprinkle your hypno-babble liberally with such gibberish. Remember you are not trying to clarify, you are trying to hypnotise!

Nominalisations are used in every day speech for the sake of brevity: we can't explain all details, we'd get nothing done. *Speech is a shorthand for experience.*

Here's some more...

'Wealth.'

'Health.'

'Attitudes.'

'Beliefs.'

'Perceptions.'

'Persuasion.' – To persuade.

'Self-esteem.' (A mythology – see book 3.)

'Confidence.'

'Fear.'

'Joy.'

'Love.'

'Happiness.'

'Experiential.'

'Wellness.'

'Disease.'

Remember the golden rule of nominalisations: *if it can't be placed into a wheel barrow or on a shelf it's probably a nominalisation. It has no sensory referents.*

As a hypnotist, nominalisations are perhaps your best friend.

Non specified comparatives.

More...

Better...

Best...

Bigger...

Faster...

Sexier...

Worst...

Fewer...

Most...

Widest...

Longest...

Less...

A minority/majority...

Improved...

Outstanding value!

Excellent!

Useless/rubbish/incompetent...

Larger numbers...

Oldest...

Youngest...

Deepest...

Lighter...

Brighter...

Progress...

With non-specified comparatives a judgement is missing. According to whom? According to whose standard and criteria? Compared to what/to whom?

Non specified verbs, people and things.

The following vague wordage can be useful to the hypno-dweeb...

Certain...feelings, people, places etc. – never specified which ones.

Some...feelings, things, times, people, events – as above!

Changes...amazing changes, change you can believe in, change now etc. – what changes did you have in mind Charley?

Places/situations/environment...Which places? Which situations? Leave it up to them!

Emotions/feelings/sensations...feelings can change, feel positive emotions! That sensation in your hand.

Behaviours...alter certain behaviours, find healthier behaviours.

Perceptions...can alter, can they not?

One/person/he/she/someone/anyone/ some people...a person can change, one can feel good. (Which person? Well your subconscious thinks YOU dummy! Remember the subconscious processes all possible meanings/interpretations. But I never directly said *you* did I!?)

Appropriate...this is a good fail safe word.

'Make the appropriate changes.'

If you asked a woman in hypnosis to feel amazing feelings she might, conceivably orgasm! Be careful what you say,

'Feel a wonderful feeling that's appropriate to your changing experience.'

'Changing experience' is beautifully ambiguous if I may say so myself. Multiple level communication there.

Advertising uses such words, not just the ones in this section: all of them, to manipulate your thoughts and actions, as do cults, religions, atheists and political groups: anyone with an agenda.

Hyperbolic words.

Some words are suggestive of extreme generalisation, a good thing for a hypnotist to know about...*real change occurs when it generalises throughout a system.*

*'**All** people feel good sometimes...'*

*'**Most** things in nature are beautiful...perhaps you'll notice the captivating colours of the clouds at sunset?'*

*'**Everywhere**, throughout your life you feel confident...'*

*'**Anyone** can learn something new...can they not?'*

*'**Everyone** has good points about them.'*

&

'I look for the good in **everyone**'...these last two commonly held beliefs can be deeply dangerous. Stalin, Lenin, Mao, Hitler, Son of Sam and other infamous serial killers had good points? Be careful what you suggest.

I like to use the truism,

'***All*** *suffering passes...*' with clients, if I deem it appropriate.

These sorts of all or nothing thinking can be the basis for depression. However some are also powerful 'meta-beliefs' on which hang the branches of potentially useful, helpful, *truly* life-affirming and healthy responses.

Hypnotic poetry: assonance and alliteration.

Hypnotic poetry is hypnotising.

Assonance = vowels sound similar.

Alliteration = consonants sound similar (the Anglo-Saxons preferred highly alliterative verse). Examples of tongue twisters are...

'Peter piper picked a peck of pickled pepper.' (Alliterative.)

'Nanny nudged Nicola.' (Both.)

'How much wood, could a wood chuck chuck, if a wood chuck could chuck wood?' (Both.)

'Hear the mellow wedding bells & try to light the fire.' (Assonance.)

As a by the by, tongue twisters can help with clarity of speech but don't overdo it.

If you can weave a bit of the old alliteration or assonance into the hypno-babble it can make it sound nice for you clients. Don't worry about it too much, just something to bear in mind. Ooh hypnotic ambiguity: bear/bare! Just knowing about these things can help you weave language with a more hypnotic rhythm and cadence. Reading good poetry will make your languaging better.

Some more languaging.

More hypno-phrases follow...

To the point where...

Americans especially like using this phrase in conversation. It is a pseudo connector phase, a false linkage saying essentially,

'X will lead to Y.'

Who says it will? In hypnosis people tend not to question such things. They are too overloaded. Talking quickly and emotionally will also overload people too as the Methodist Wesley knew only too well. Beware! I digress, anyway...

*'You can **relax in trance** to the point where nothing else seems important for a while, you know that feeling?'*

*'Allow a wave of comfort to spread from head to toe to the point where you **feel blissful.**'*

*'It's funny how some people **enter trance** to the point where going even deeper just seems the right thing to do.'*

What's it like when...

This is a command to re-member/re-experience something.

*'What's it like when you **relax?**'*

*'What's it like when you **daydream?**'*

*'What's it like when you **feel very attractive?**'*

*'What's it like when you **have total self-belief, now?**'*

Perceive...

Often used in media reports. Used to undermine and cast doubt upon. *The implication of the word perceive is that reality is plastic, nothing is real, everyone's point of view is valid.* Don't you ever believe it! By the way anyone who says there is no such thing as absolute truth is making a statement about absolute truth. Examples,

'Some people perceive that crime is rising.'

'Some people perceive the President doesn't seem as powerful as he once did.'

'You perceive x,y,z.'

In hypnosis you can say...

'With new perspectives feeling can change.'

'As new facts come to light our perception can alter, can't it?'

'Three people witnessing the same event will perceive it quite differently.'

'Some perspectives are more helpful than others.'

You get the idea. These are reframes. You can use this word like any word in a useful fashion or not. When people are told their valid perceptions of reality are insane or just not true when they actually are, this is known as 'gaslighting' from the film of the same name. It is a form of mental torture and used in psychological warfare.

New…

Since the end of the so-called Middle Ages the word **New** has been associated with 'good,' 'progressive.' But is it? Good and progressive according to whom? The 'New' has led to the destruction of many time-honoured traditions and norms.

New washing powder!

New Labour! New Deal!

New this, new that.

New Year New You!

The New Age (which is ancient paganism???!).

This tiny three letter word has an almost magical power over human minds. It shouldn't. However as a hypnotist you may well find some use for it. After I have almost completed all therapeutic changes I sometimes say,

'Look at that new you in the mirror with all the confidence, self-worth and self-belief you desire, the you you always really are and were deep inside etc...'

I then ask them to step into their 'new self' and to feel how it feels.

Power...

Why is it always implied that something is good because it's powerful?

'Learn powerful techniques!'

'Zitto has the power to kill all acne!'

'Powerfully increase your success with women!'

'Knowledge is power.'

'She was a powerful woman.'

'A powerfully intoxicating aroma.'

As a hypnotist stop taking words for granted: like a writer they are your bread and butter. *Don't be afraid to invent words and word combos or deliberately use bad grammar.*

'Power play!'

'Powerful changes!'

'Power to heal...blah, blah...'

'The power of your subconscious mind.'

'Empowered!' One of the worst words in human history. Meaningless twaddle loved by con men and B-S artists everywhere. Self-help gurus will lull dopey and desperate folk with siren promises of 'unlimited power.' Thankfully humans are incapable of having unlimited power.

Just...

Means **only do this**, **don't do anything but**...it focuses and narrows options –

'...just relax...'

'Just in time.'

'Just focus on your little finger.'

Only...

Another option of the above...

'Only pleasant feelings take you deeper.'

Both these seemingly small words are potentially highly hypnotic as they can be used to narrow the attention.

Yet...

Temporal predicate...

'You don't feel good YET.'

'You haven't changed YET.'

'You haven't seen the yeti, YET.'

Implication? It will happen. It is about to.

Seems very innocent too.

'I know you haven't relaxed all the way down yet.' (But you will!)

Similar to *but*...one train of thought is interrupted and attention is redirected.

But

Whatever went before is totally negated.

'You felt bad BUT things change, feelings change.'

'You said x,y,z BUT a,b,c can also happen.'

'Tension can make you feel bad BUT we all relax sooner or later...'

If...

A word of possibilities. Highly hypnotic as in 'what if' used to stimulate the imagination and in worrying.

'***If*** *you relax deeply you can feel better.'*

'***If*** *you change today what will the benefits be?'*

'***If*** *you exercise how much better will you feel?'*

Wonder...

An indirect command to DAYDREAM!

'I wonder how your unconscious will solve that problem?'

'You can wonder...in trance.'

We 'wonder and wander' in our minds when we drift into dolly daydreams.

Ponder...

An indirect command to go inside and daydream, gently reflect on things. <u>Real meditation is when we simply and pleasantly follow a train of thought.</u> That is, when we ponder things. A good form of relaxed rumination; in order to do it we – go inside.

'As you ponder the change you want and it can be secret change...'

'Ponder, really ponder...'

'Pondering upon where you'd like this personal process to go...'

So and so said...

The infamous *'quotes pattern'* it should be called 'expertise hijacking' or the 'sneaky influence' pattern. You can also use it to dissociate something from yourself by attributing it to another even though you said it.

'Dr. Bumstew said, 'relaxing deeply is good.'

Speed seduction 'hypnotists' say things like,

'...This man walked up to her and said, 'imagine the two of us having wild sex!'

You put the thought you want the person to think into someone else's mouth.

'Dr. Milton Erickson, the great hypnotist said...my voice can go with you, like the sound of the breeze in the trees.'

We often do this in normal conversation to sound authoritative: we repeat what we read in a newspaper, we quote from a statistical 'factoid' etc. *All hypnosis uses normal and everyday conversational patterns.* The less hypnosis seems like hypnosis the better. Tobacco companies used to use this principle to advertise cigarettes, a quack and no doubt outrageously paid 'Doctor' in a white lab coat smokes a cigarette and says, 'Hmmm good healthy tobacco,' while smiling.

Or...

'Or you got it, or you ain't!' as Zero Mostel said. OR = double bind. The illusion of choice.

*'Do you want to go into trance now **or** later?'* (Either way you're going down!)

*'Is your left foot **or** right hand most relaxed now?'* (Presupposes relaxation too. This also produces a 'split' in consciousness. Focusing on two things at once produces overload – trance is the only escape!)

*'Do you want to tidy your room before **or** after lunch?'*

*'Will you vote left **or** right wing in the election?'* Notice only two choices – a duad – one up on a one party state. Hmmm?

Associational networks.

The human mind works via association. You can hypnotise just by getting people to re-associate or associate to something hypnotic. In a first hypnosis session I almost always say something as simple as,

*'You can follow your own associative processes to these words can you not? Like the word **'comfort'** and follow where it leads you...'*

Let's break this seemingly innocent little remark down.

'You can follow...' (The beginning of an indirect suggestion: 'follow' what?)

'...your own *associative processes* to these words... (The key words here are: 'associative processes' – what does this mean? Haven't a clue!)

'...can you not?' (Tag question: a negation softener for the above command. The whole statement above is also a truism so is not rejected. It is a fact that we do follow trains of thought triggered by certain words – and when we do we enter trance!)

'Like the word comfort and follow where it leads you.' (Here you suggest and you are only a hypnotist and it's only a suggestion that the listener 'follow' their train of associations for the word 'comfort.' Trance is comfortable number one and two what will the mind search for? Feelings, memories, other words, ideas, concepts associated with that word. If you said 'knife' a whole lot of other associations would be elicited. I am sure few would be good. Remember: hypnosis is an amplifying state as I said in book one, 'How to hypnotise anyone,' – be careful where you send the brain!)

In book 3: 'Powerful Hypnosis,' I will teach you how to do 'trance hijacking.'

Ambiguity and confusion.

English is a very ambiguous language. That is, it has many words that that have multiple meanings, it has many words that mean more than one thing. Why? Modern English is actually composed of three or four languages: Old English (the pre Norman Conquest Germanic dialect), Norman French and Latin. There's also some Old Norse in there but that again is a Germanic tongue. A valley in southern England is a dale in the North.

Now ambiguity is hypnotic. Why? When things are ambiguous and open to interpretation the meaning is unclear, our old hypnotic friend vagueness again, and *the brain searches for all possible meanings at an unconscious level.*

Examples:

'Hear/here…' - *'…you can hear my voice, here and now…'*

A confusing way of saying, 'Listen.' Here and hear??? Brain goes on search for meaning – mini trance established. The person has to 'go inside' to make sense of what you said. NLP calls this a 'transderivational search.' I call it a 'search for meaning.' Also if a person hears a generalised statement such as,

'A person can learn,'

the person's mind will at one level think it means them, that **they** are the person being referred to – known as a 'lack of a referential indices.'

Remember the subconscious mind can and does process all possible meanings. So how can we put these principles to any use? By the way it is possible to make a sentence have many possible permutation and meanings. A statement could have up to four or five possible interpretations. So beware of sales people and politicians (just another type of sales person) who might say things like,

*'And so you, **like me**, are probably thinking what's the best choice etc...'*

An ambiguous hidden command: LIKE ME!!! Politicians use this one all the time: listen out for it. Multiple meanings – 'like me' as in, 'Have the same point of view and LIKE ME I'm nice!' Scumbags!

How about,

'**By now**, *you might be wondering which product is best for your needs...*'

Hold on let's rewind that nugget...

'BUY NOW...you might...' A covert command to BUY THE PRODUCT NOW.

Another one they use is,

'...and by and by,'

Seemingly innocent, actually a command to BUY!!! By and BUY! Geddit!? Devious, devious secondary psychopaths out there folks. No morals.

Another one for hypnosis...

'Entrance/in trance...now.'

Another favourite of politicians is the word, 'Look!' They will say,

'**Look.** The opposition is saying this because blah, blah, lie, blah, lie.'

Now what did they do? They just gave you a command to LOOK at them. That is fixate your attention on them. Prime Ministers, Presidents and politicians use this a lot. Beware of charmers with dead, shark like eyes.

In hypnosis I use this phrase...

'You can notice words, and you can notice noticing words, and as you notice noticing words you can relax...'

This is a confusing way of saying: 'listen and relax.' The ambiguity produces trance. *The confused conscious brain is so overloaded with potential meanings it 'escapes' into a trance state.* I sometimes use this for activating amnesia so that a person's conscious mind doesn't interfere and try to analyse everything afterwards,

'You can forget to remember, what you can remember to forget!'

Or

'You don't have to remember. The important thing is to have certain experiences naturally recorded in your mind. Their presence has been and will be of service to you. It's nice to though that they are there, unconsciously, now...'

Analysis of above

'You don't have to remember...' ('You don't have' to pattern – what am I saying by implication? FORGET!)

'...the important thing...' (Implication: it's not important to remember)

'...is to have certain experiences...' (Which ones? By the way trust that the person's subconscious will derive the right meaning for them. It knows more than you or they – consciously – do.)

'...naturally recorded in your mind. Their presence has been and will be of service to you...' ('Naturally recorded' implies – you learnt it all easily and it's already there. 'Has been/will be': temporal predicates/also mildly confusing – past and future covered very quickly.)

'...It's nice to know they are there, unconsciously.' (If you are unconscious of something you are unaware of it; like when you FORGET! Plus - the 'changes' are automatically wired in.)

'...now.' (Command: do it all right now please

Mr. Subconscious or whatever you are!)

Hopefully you are now learning how this can be used by you, don't overdo it: prolonged confusion is unpleasant, a little bit is fine and matches the natural experience of learning new things when we often feel a bit confused; and most importantly you are now *aware* of how powerful people will use this stuff against you and yours. If you are aware you can notice it consciously – so it won't program you surreptitiously.

The fails person.

As an amusing story I thought I'd just tell you how a dumb sales person tried to use NLP on me. I can't even remember what the twit was selling but he immediately started asking me...

'Is this something you agree with?'

'Do you like x,'

'Is it ok to y?'

He was asking me questions unrelated to his product to establish a **'yes set.'**

An example would be,

'Do you like nice things?

Well who the f%$* doesn't!??

Anyway as he did this I failed to answer any of his questions just saying,

'Dunno...'

'You don't know?!' he replied.

My responses agitated him a bit: the sales techniques weren't working! He started flipping a chart with pictures as you'd find in a children's picture book (**hypnotic age regression**), beside the pictures were simple sentences saying,

'Imagine having this product...'

He was talking while showing these picture/slogan things on a flip chart/booklet ('Imagine' is a hypnotic word -see book 1, talking and flipping the chart - trying to overload consciousness, pictorial suggestions offered to peripheral vision: outside of foveal awareness or 'central vision' and thus subliminal.)

Ok I'd had enough of the dopey monkey by this

point and said,

'Are you trying to use a yes set on me?'

He froze. I had interrupted his pattern. He had no response available and went into a startled trance: you know the deer in headlight type.

'I, er, what?' he stuttered.

'I am a Master Hypnotist (I'm not!)," I said ominously, 'Don't ever try to use that crap on me again. People like me invented that s%*t! Go and try that with someone else...'

I looked at him smiling and knowingly, as though looking at a subordinate, or a naughty child. He smiled nervously, mumbled something stupid and left. You see the emperor never has any clothes.

Sales people are by and large pond scum: I like to play with them. If they ask you lots of questions ask tons back and dominate the conversation. Often they will call you 'friend,' 'mate,' 'buddy.' These people have no friends, they want your hard earned cash, they enjoy manipulating people! Now YOU can do it to them.

Adverbs to tell people what to think and feel.

Use 'ly' ending adverbs in hypnosis. How many times have you heard some lying lowlife of a politician say something like,

*'I **fundamentally** disagree with the Right Honourable prat opposite...'*

*'Are you **seriously** suggesting that the best economic policy is to sell water to fish?'*

Many politicians' and corporate bosses' favourite nominalisation is,

*'I **passionately** believe...*(insert mad idea)*!'*

The key words here are: **passionately** and **believe**. As if *believing* something to be true and being *passionate* about it was a justification for anything! You are free of course to passionately believe anything: you may well believe you are the Cheese god of Mars; however what happened to important things like evidence, logic and proof? And if you were passionate about something wouldn't it be self-evident? Hitler passionately believed many insane things: was he therefore right?

*'I **honestly** did not go to kinky sex parties at the tax payer's expense...'*

(Whichever lying two-faced politician you like might say something like this eventually; usually anti-corruption 'Tsars.')

Adverbs modify verbs - action words; they give us its quality.

'Happily, undemocratically, theoretically, wonderfully, jokingly, deceptively etc...'

<u>These adverbs are used to tell people how to **think, feel and will** about something and so direct what they **should** do.</u>

You can use it in hypnosis like this,

*'You can go **deeply** into trance...'* (How do you go into trance? Deeply of course!)

*'You can feel **deliciously** relaxed...'* (Relax = verb: what do you want your client to do? Relax, how so? Deliciously of course! The adverb modifies the verb – it tells you how to *do* the verb. What does deliciously mean in reality? Let the person's subconscious fill in the gaps. One person's idea of delicious is not another's. Also note that 'delicious' is a sensual

word. I will cover 'hypnotic sensual language' in book 3.)

*'You can **delightfully** make just the right changes and it can be secret change.'*

Don't make 'change' difficult or unpleasant make it a happy shift!

Not now but soon! How to construct 'deepeners.'

The formula for constructing a deepener is this:

1. Tell someone you are going to do something soon. Not right now but in just a short time ahead.

2. Tell them that when you say or do a trigger activity or phrase that their hypnotic trance will deepen.

3. Ask them if that's ok rhetorically. That is, assume it is.

4. Go ahead and activate the trigger.

Remember the varieties of the most hypnotic sentence…

'Not now but soon…not now but in a moment…not yet but soon…in a few seconds…before I/you…'

The Silly Hypnotic Deepener.

'In a few moments not just yet

I'll say the names of three fruits

and with the sound of each word

you can go 50 times deeper into trance and hypnosis.

You ready? Ok? (Don't wait for a response.)

Banana…deeper…and deeper…50 times deeper…

Apple…even deeper than that…50 times deeper into…

your own state of hypnosis and trance…

and one more for luck…

Pineapple!

Deeper and deeper still,

all the way down

into

deep, hypnotic…

SLEEP!'

<u>What the trigger is doesn't matter. You set up an **expectation** that something will happen on the trigger, the subconscious automatically does</u>

the rest. The power of expectation will be dealt with thoroughly in book 3.

You could click your fingers. Tap their knee/shoulder. You could fart on cue! You can say go 5, 10, 15, 100 times deeper – what does that even mean? It's all nonsense.

To deepen hypnotic trance you can also get people to imagine that they are going upward, down, through* or *into* *something.

You can get people to imagine going to a special place and falling asleep. News programmes often draw people in as do TV shows and films by the camera travelling along, known as 'dollying' away from the screen as though pulling you deeper into the imaginary world. That's a deepener dummy! Sky TV in England does it right at the beginning of the program just after commercial breaks.

You can really get creative with deepeners. See the appendix for your special personal use copyright free bonus: 'The Unicorn Deepener.'

Embedded commands hypnotic induction.

In this example I am using embedded commands to induce trance. *Notice I am talking about the experience of hypnosis. By so doing the listener makes sense of what I say by experiencing it.* Easy.

Oh I will give you another way to deliver embeds successfully. You can lower your tonality – the command tone at the end of a sentence, and you can whisper the command (book 1 covers this in detail) AND *you can turn your head either up or down or left or right as you say the embed! The subconscious will notice on what words you turn your head and act on them.* Subtle and sneaky. Many examples of hypnotic language are covered in this induction. See if you can spot them yourself. Be thorough in your analysis.

The Embedded Command induction.

(Remember to use your relaxed hypnotic tone from book 1.)

'Ok just close your eyes and

listen at some level...

The thing about hypnosis is that

*you don't have to **relax deeply** to do it...*

some people pay attention to their breathing...

some people notice bodily sensations they usually ignore

*others find as they **go into a trance***

that it's just like when

you're daydreaming.

So the thing is I don't know how

you experience hypnosis

everyone is different.

We all have different responses.

You might think that it's going to be like

*a stage hypnotist's show where he says **sleep!***

And the person can instantly

***fall into a very deep...hypnotic trance**,*

but trance isn't like that

*some people **go into trance***

while driving down a motorway

*they travel five miles and **ponder** how they got there...*

Because they knew how to drive.

*That is **you're unconscious** knew*

*and so your mind was free to **wonder...***

and wander...

It's not even necessary to

experience feelings of comfort

*to **enter this state**.*

It's like when you watch TV

and what you are watching is so interesting that

you become fascinated

by the imaginary reality of the story you are watching.

*And we **experience hypnosis***

*when we **feel utterly absorbed***

by an enjoyable activity.

It happens, does it not?

Did you ever **feel an intense state of fascination**

about something captivating?

We all do, from time to time, now.

So you see trance is something everyone has experienced...

there are times when you have **become totally absorbed***, are there not?*

In trance things just seem to **slow...right...down...**

as a person goes deeper and deeper inside

into that trance of their unconscious mind...

Even your perception of time can alter, now...

A woman told me her hypnotic experience was one

in which she did indeed **feel very calm**

that she went on a journey

into the world of her imagination

*as we do when we **dream**...*

*and **learn**, really learn.*

And as she did that

she sat still and quiet

as I watched from the outside...

The changes in her breathing

the way the pulse on her foot had

slowed...right down...

Those changes are standard

in trance.

*I said '**go inside'***

and I don't even know what that means

but

*it was as though she took a nice **rest***

*And did she **drift in a reverie**?*

Who knows?

We all have our own way

as I said

of experiencing hypnosis.

But I know this...

*we all **go into a profoundly deep state of hypnosis***

when the time is right, now.

*This is your chance to **feel entranced**.*

Trance is the learning state in which

you learn effortlessly.

That state we've all experienced

*where we could **focus intently***

on what had captivated our attention

*so that we can **ignore things that aren't important***

just for a while...

It's nice to know everyone has that ability,

is it not?'

Awakening...

(In an energised voice!)

And now you have completed your journey...

You can on my count of 1-3 return to full waking consciousness

feeling great...

And 1 – aware of your body, environment and noises...

And 2 – feeling almost **wide awake**...

unnecessary relaxation leaving your body...

All doubts and negativity washed away...

feeling re-energised and good...

And as soon as you are ready...

You can open your eyes on 3...

Fully back to full waking consciousness,

Feeling alert!'

Embeds that induce trance.

You can put embedded commands into any conversation: I advise you don't. Milton Erickson had a secretary with recurring migraines take dictation for him. As he dictated the letter he placed embedded commands in the text and the woman's headache vanished. He also used embedded commands with patients in mental health wards: he mimicked their insane word salad and he embedded commands for good health within them. Patients recovered. The following can be put in ANY conversation...always use with good intention and caution.

'Calm down.'

'Feel good.'

'Relax.'

'Notice x.' (Body part, feeling, images etc.)

'Rest.'

'Drift.'

'Become absorbed.'

'Focus inwardly.'

'Relax deeply.'

'Relax deeper.'

'Relax comfortably.'

'Enter hypnosis.'

'Go into trance.'

'Go inside.'

'Peace.'

'Gently.'

'Softly.'

'Quietly.'

'Be still.'

'Relax very deeply.'

'Start relaxing…'

'You are so calm/relaxed.'

'Unwind.'

'Feel comfort.'

'Feel calm.'

'Feel relaxed.'

'You become hypnotised.'

'You drift into a trance.'

'You fall into hypnosis.'

'You drift off.'

'Go into a pleasant relaxed trance.'

'Experience trance.'

'Breathing calmly.'

'Feeling so relaxed.'

'Rest very deeply.'

'Draw your attention/focus to x.' ('X' being whatever you like.)

'Begin to relax.'

'Relax even deeper.'

'Relax without effort.'

'Automatically relax.'

'Spontaneously relax.'

'Calm.'

'Release that tension.'

'Feel tranquil.'

'Feel so comfortable.'

'Rest soundly.'

'You're drifting down.'

'Breathe comfortably.'

'Slow...right...down.'

'Let go.'

'Feel growing/spreading relaxation.'

'Calming.'

'Soothing.'

'Relaxing.' (suffix 'ing' = a process that is occurring now.)

'X can increase.' ('X' being calm, comfort, relaxation.)

'Notice certain things changing.'

'Become aware of that pleasant feeling/sensation.'

'Become fascinated.'

'Become mesmerised.'

'Be mesmerised.'

'Have you ever been mesmerised by something?'

'Pay attention to x.' ('X' being your voice, feet, whatever.)

'You're unconscious.'

'In trance.'

'Feel fascination.'

'Become enthralled.'

To practise write down some paragraphs in which you have embedded little phraselets like the ones above. Better still make up your own. The principles are obvious are they not?

Describing a state revivifies it.

What does state x feel like? Imagine you have a big juicy lemon in front of you. Look at it glistening and gleaming, a beautiful spanking yellow. It looks so juicy and moist. You slice it in half. The lemony juices roll out. The fruit sparkles in the sunlight: you take a big juicy bite!

And perhaps you salivated reading that? *Words alone can evoke powerful psychophysiological responses.* They can stir the emotions: think of Churchill's rousing war speeches. 'We shall fight them on the beeches...we shall never surrender!' He had obviously studied the ancient art of rhetoric.

Describing trance and hypnosis can and will evoke it. No formal induction is needed – you just sound like you're having a normal conversation. Some examples of what you could do follow...

Driving trance.

'Have you ever been driving along a motorway/freeway and before you knew it you had completely zoned out and gone into a

*daydream? So you'd travelled 5 miles or so on autopilot. Because you know how to drive – **you're unconscious** did it for you, leaving you free to **wander off mentally**. Funny isn't it?'*

Reading trance.

*'What's it like when you're reading a book and it's so interesting that you **become completely absorbed** in it? So you just completely **ignore your surroundings**. You just **become so fascinated** by the characters, the imaginary landscape, all the exciting events and you feel emotions intensely in that state, don't you. You see when you're reading in that absorbed way – **you're in hypnosis...now**. And your sense of time passing changes too doesn't it. Focusing on the words generates pictures in your mind, compelling pictures that captivate you for a while.'*

TV trance.

*'Do you know that you can **go into trance** watching TV? As long as you are really into the program. It's not like **going into hypnosis** where your attention is focused inside. It's an external state of focus. You **become so***

absorbed *by the TV, the characters, maybe you find one really attractive and can't take your eyes off them. You **become very relaxed and still** too. Maybe the photography or spectacle of the movie is so incredible that you **forget what's going on around you for a while**. You ever **feel that**? **Now**, I'm like that when I watch Star Wars. What films make you **enter that state?**'*

Conversational trance.

*'We've all had conversations in which we **become totally absorbed**, haven't we? Maybe someone is really funny or interesting or very attractive and we **listen to every word**, we **ignore everything else**…sometimes it's what the person is talking about that can mesmerise someone, sometimes it's a quality of their voice, a certain cadence, an attractive quality, maybe the resonance that can really allow you to **focus in** and **relax** while listening.'*

I'm laying it on thick to illustrate a point. You can be more subtle if you wish.

You could describe playing golf and going into

the zone, sex, anything in which you become very absorbed – it's very easy to do. You just need to practise. _If you want someone to feel a state – say joy – describe it vividly – a time it happened to you...when you do this skilfully the listener will experience it too._ Don't be afraid to be flowery, somewhat. Notice what I compare the feeling to – this is a metaphor, which is hypnotic.

'I remember a time when I passed an audition to get into drama school I was so happy afterwards, I knew it was a moment that would change my life. I felt this lovely warm glow in my head, a kind of lightness, a soft tingle, it felt like a nice warm sun inside me...making me feel good.'

Over the top I know. By doing this you are also triggering associations to what you are saying in _their_ past experience. This is one way humans bond.

Or relaxation.

'Your muscles just **let go** don't they, gradually all the tension eases away. You just **rest** maybe lying down or sitting. Sometimes you get a soft *sweet feeling in your muscles too. You might **drift off into a daydream**. Before you know it your whole body can **feel very calm and deeply relaxed**...we've all experienced that.'*

Interestingly when women see men they are attracted too they feel a set of feelings inside. Often these are tingles or butterflies. *If you talk about something you evoke it.* Then you can change it into a colour or symbol – intensify it or move it about. Odd isn't it??

Your 1st bonus: Symbolic deepeners.

This is a nice alternative to the PMR or an addition to it. *It allows the person to use their own **symbolism** to relax the muscles.* You can also use it to elicit pleasurable feelings. Now why on earth would you do that!? Deep hypnosis is assumed but it would work in light trance too. Let's also assume the feeling I am referring to is relaxation. It can be anything! *Remember symbols are very powerful; more powerful than you know. They affect the deepest instincts, templates and archetypes of the 'unconscious mind.'*

The Symbolic Deepener script.

(Hypnosis is assumed.)

'Be aware of this feeling,

this relaxation you're feeling. Now...

***Imagine**...*

if you were to form your symbol of deep relaxation...

in your mind.

See it there...

Wherever there is?

Get to know that symbol,

Where is it?

How big is it?

Really know it.

Now, take your symbol

and let it have a colour...

if you haven't already.

A colour that represents this amazing feeling...

Now,

when you're ready...

just let that colourful symbol...

liquefy, dissolve into some part of you...

taking this feeling with it...

this deep, healing relaxation...

spreading

into

some part of your body...

Enjoy these wonderful feelings as they soak into

are absorbed by that place...

Very deeply so...

Now, move it somewhere else

it would do you good...

As you do,

these good feelings

and more...

only increase in intensity...

Feel them intensify!

That's right...

so that pleasurable feeling

only increases.

Maybe it pulsates

or throbs nicely

or maybe it moves in waves

or twirls

or circulates...

or radiates

from that place...

outward

and inward...

I don't know...

It's your experience...

And again...

let your colourful symbol

liquefy, dissolve into

another part of your deserving body...

Just the right place...

You know where is best...

As it melts,

these good feelings can increase...

double,

triple,

quadruple...

if you like,

*if **you're unconscious** is willing...*

Now take this lovely healing feeling...

and

allow it to

feel even more pleasant

as you notice it travel

somewhere else,

wherever you need it...

taking the feelings with it

into another part of you...

bathing your

mind-body system

with wonderful feelings...

And so,

the more intense

this blissful feeling does become

the more you enjoy it...

with each breath

the feeling only gets better,

healing you

in some mysterious way...

taking you

deeper and deeper into

deep hypnotic - SLEEP!

Let that colourful symbol

liquefy, dissolve into some other

part of your mind...

your body...

soothing,

healing,

refreshing

each and both of you, now...

Let that feeling

spread into every part of

that body right now...

I'll be quiet for 30 seconds

and in that time

and you have all the time

you need in trance...

to do this...

that's right...

Experiencing all

these wonderful feelings...

let them double,

triple in intensity,

quadruple in intensity...

until you have moved it down

along,

up,

throughout,

your increasingly peaceful mind and body...

Let that colourful symbol

liquefy

become absorbed

by all the parts of you...

that need,

deserve,

can have these wonderful feelings,

now...

That's it...

Feel this process occurring in the pause/pores...'

(Be quiet for 30 seconds as they do it.)

Your new language power!

Now you have learned many things about the power of language and your improving ability to use it, have you not? You will have many more choices of how to construct your own hypnotic inductions now. But there is more!

In my next book I will teach you more hypnosis secrets, I promise I'll give you many more options of how to hypnotise people and send them into pleasurable oblivion which will give you real flexibility and we'll start to delve into what to do once someone is hypnotised! I will start to give you my own powerful techniques for doing hypnotherapy: the interventions, how to construct suggestions, what subconscious rejection is, the reasons why hypnotists have any clients at all...you see I have so much knowledge to share, about hypnosis and how the mind really works, what the placebo effect really is, maybe I'll talk about the difference between men and women's brains, perhaps about how carefully calculated manipulation is carried out by 'influential groups' in society using NLP, hypnotic principles, powerful psychological conditioning techniques and more against you and yours (oops I've said too much!), if you're good...all done in the same fun, informal way of course.

I've just decided in book 3 I will teach you at least two bonus modules...

How to pass any personality test with flying colours.

How to do 'psychic' cold reading.

The first two books have already given you a very thorough understanding of hypnosis, by reading them you are ahead of the pack; so if you've enjoyed the ride so far, join me for more hypnotic whistleblowing in book 3 – 'Powerful Hypnosis!' Are you ready for level 3 my Padawan apprentice!???!

Wishing you every success...and you will succeed.

Don't forget your 'Unicorn Deepener' bonus awaits at the end of the appendices!

Appendix 1: PMR script.

'Ok just close your eyes...

and just pay attention to your breathing...

in and out... (time this on the in and out breath – thereby 'pacing' the client's reality.)

That's right...

You don't have to change your breathing at all...

Just notice it...

Draw all of your attention to your breathing...

as you **relax deeply**...

Now,

just focus your attention on the top of your head...

your scalp...

Imagine you simply **relax**

all the muscles in the top of your head...

Relax your forehead...

Calming...yourself...**down**...

all the way down...

Good...

And now...

Your eyes...

Your temples...

Relaxing...

Your ears can relax...

the back of your head too,

supported by that pillow/cushion...

so comfortable...

Again **relax all the** tiny **muscles**

around your eyelids...

all of them

can just **let go,**

relax and unwind, now...

The muscles between your eyebrows

can soften,

smooth out...

take a **rest**.

And even the nose can relax,

tension can accumulate around the nose

but it **can melt away** now too...

And who knows, (phonetic ambiguity: nose/knows.)

how the nose

knows how to relax?

But it does...

And female rabbits are known as does/**doze**... (confusion: non sequitur – 'doze' = command - sleep!)

And you can

effortlessly...

allow this feeling of

pure relaxation

to spread down your neck...

That's right...

so wonderfully relaxed,

peace increasing...

inside...your mind...

because...

as **your body relaxes,**

your mind relaxes...

does it not?

Time to just **slow...things...down...** (Anxiety is associated with speed. Suggest the opposite. 'Down' also suggestive of going down into hypnosis.)

down to your shoulders...

Just let those shoulders...

relax comfortably.

Don't have to do anything...

for a while...

The back muscles,

releasing past tension.

That old...

tension just melts away...

so pleasant...

that calming, soothing, restful sensation

spreading...

all the way down

your lower back

increasing **serenity**, (single word command)

relaxing,

smoothing out certain things...

almost as though,

someone you love deeply

is massaging

all that old tightness you had away.

Your chest and tummy muscles...

feeling so soft,

so wonderful.

That feeling can spread

to where it needs to go.

Just getting rid of any

unnecessary tension,

in the past...now.

And down to your

waste/waist area, (phonetic ambiguity)

feeling

tranquility, now...

And what's the most wonderful thing

about kindness and love?

For yourself too? (Whispered)

Letting those big thigh muscles

relax so pleasantly,

that chair comfortably supporting...

your hamstrings muscles too.

Your arms can relax.

The deltoids,

biceps,

triceps,

the forearms...

all the way down

to your hands,

your palms relaxing...

each finger and thumb...

so comfort-able...

Aware of the feeling

of your interlaced fingers,

the feeling of your jeans...(whatever they are wearing)

any textures...

the different feelings,

in both hands.

One hand might feel slightly lighter,

And the other slighter warmer... (truism – this is often the case.)

And I don't know which hand is the right hand

And which one is left. (Phonetic ambiguity/double meaning for left and right.)

Perhaps...

your calves can

relax next...

your shins,

your Achilles tendons...

down to your ankles,

top of your feet,

aware of the feeling of the shoes/socks etc. (if they are wearing any) on those feet...

your toes too...

each toe relaxing,

one...

by...

one...

And your sole/soul... (phonetic ambiguity suggestive of 'deep rooted' relaxation)

deeply relaxed.

Your entire mind and body

deeply relaxed, now.

Now I just want for a moment...

to speak to...

you're unconscious (ambiguity – your/you're)

I'd like to thank that part...

that was and is protecting you...

looking out for you...

that was making you

too worried,

stressed,

overly tense...

back then.

But now I would like,

the sympathetic part of the nervous system;

that's the part that takes care

of the arousal phase of the 'fight or flight' response

to **calm down, now**...

to allow the parasympathetic phase,

of the nervous system;

that is the **calming down** phase...

to begin to predominate, now...

Only responding to *real* danger,

when needed.

The old overly tense and stressed pattern,

is unnecessary, now...

That's right.'

Appendix 2: Conscious and Unconscious Dissociation script.

'As a part of you listens another part becomes more and more immersed in this process...

Maybe one part wants to follow what is happening, while another in fact knows without effort and simply absorbs things...

Perhaps a part may be concentrated on some ideas yet at the same time another can continue on its journey into the inner world of experiences...

A part can doubt and question and another can accept positive change and experience is possible, can understand with more and more trust...

Maybe some part wants to observe and be alert whereas another uncovers its own creative potentials and deeply desires to try something new...

One part may try to exert too much control over everything with its learnt bias, while another deeper part of you is free to imagine some things you desire and put into practise...

A part is preoccupied by the moment as another simply finds it easy to go down stream and act on certain things that please it most...'

Appendix 3: The Silly Hypnotic Deepener.

'In a few moments not just yet

I'll say the names of three fruits

and with the sound of each word

you can go 50 times deeper into trance and hypnosis.

You ready? Ok? (Don't wait for a response.)

Banana...deeper...and deeper...50 times deeper...

Apple...even deeper than that...50 times deeper into

your own state of hypnosis and trance...

And one more for luck...

Pineapple!

Deeper and deeper still,

all the way down

into...

deep, hypnotic...

SLEEP!'

Appendix 4: 1st Bonus - The Symbolic Deepener.

'Be aware of this feeling,

this relaxation you're feeling. Now...

Imagine...

if you were to form your symbol of deep relaxation...

in your mind.

See it there...

Wherever there is?

Get to know that symbol,

Where is it?

How big is it?

Really know it.

Now, take your symbol

and let it have a colour...

if you haven't already.

A colour that represents this amazing feeling...

Now,

When you're ready…

just let that colourful symbol…

liquefy, dissolve into some part of you…

taking this feeling with it…

this deep, healing relaxation…

spreading

into

some part of your body…

Enjoy these wonderful feelings as they soak into,

are absorbed by that place…

Very deeply so…

Now, move it somewhere else

it would do you good…

As you do,

these good feelings

and more...

only increase in intensity...

Feel them intensify!

That's right...

so that pleasurable feeling

only increases.

Maybe it pulsates

or throbs nicely

or maybe it moves in waves

or twirls

or circulates...

or radiates

from that place...

outward

and inward...

I don't know...

It's your experience...

And again...

let your colourful symbol

liquefy, dissolve into

another part of your deserving body...

Just the right place...

Move it there...

you know where is best...

As it melts,

these good feelings can increase...

double,

triple,

quadruple...

if you like,

if you're unconscious is willing...

Now take this lovely healing feeling...

and

allow it to

feel even more pleasant

as you notice it travel

somewhere else,

wherever you need it...

taking the feelings with it

into another part of you...

bathing your

mind-body system

with wonderful feelings...

And so,

the more intense

this blissful feeling does become

the more you enjoy it...

with each breath

the feeling only gets better,

healing you

in some mysterious way...

taking you

deeper and deeper into

deep hypnotic - **SLEEP!**

Let that colourful symbol

liquefy, dissolve into some other

part of your mind...

your body...

soothing,

healing,

refreshing

each and both of you, now...

Move it where it needs to go.

Let that feeling

spread into every part of

that body right now...

I'll be quiet for 30 seconds

and in that time

and you have all the time

you need in trance…

to do this…

that's right…

experiencing all

these wonderful feelings…

let them double,

triple in intensity,

quadruple in intensity…

until you have moved it down

along,

up,

throughout,

your increasingly peaceful mind and body…

Let that colourful symbol

liquefy

become absorbed

by all the parts of you...

that need,

deserve,

can have these wonderful feelings,

now...

That's it...

Feel this process occurring in the pause/pores...'

(Be quiet for 30 seconds.)

Appendix 5: 2nd Bonus Deepener - The Unicorn Deepener.

(Hypnosis is assumed – I usually use this on a second or third session – you can however use it whenever you wish and adapt it for all purposes even stage hypnosis. The purpose of the script is to get the 'dreaming mind' to function/take over – this is the part that causes hypnotic change to become real.)

'Imagine a flying unicorn of great beauty

and only positive intention...

A guide,

a helper...

or some other benevolent dream being...

from the land of myth and legend...

from the most creative part

of who you truly, deeply are...

that will allow you to

travel **all the way down**

into the deepest and most profound levels

of deep hypnosis and deep trance

that it is possible for you to go to today.

And **you're unconscious** knows just where that is...

On the count of **'3-2-1 SLEEP!'**

you will travel down

with this guide's assistance

and inner journeying

into dreams and deep,

profound...

hypnotic ...

SLEEP!

SLEEP!

Deeper down with each number I count down...

and on 1

you will be as deep as it is possible

for you to go today –

deeply hypnotised,

deeply entranced...

in **deep hypnotic SLEEP!**

Sleep, peace in deep sleep!

Floating, flying, drifting into dreams...

and an entranced sleep,

down you go with your guide,

your guardian

that takes you down to exactly where you need to go...

On **'3!'**

Passing down through to the deepest

and most truly profound levels

of hypnosis and trance

where anything realistic, positive and healthy

can be made manifest,

to the place inside where all

amazing change occurs,

a place where you believe

the change you desire can happen.

Deeper and deeper down now,

'2!'...even deeper down, now...

almost at the deepest levels of your mind,

perhaps THE deepest,

where all powerful and positive change

can only happen for you...

deeper and deeper down now,

all the way down

to truly a DEEPER MAGIC

in your mind,

an ancient wisdom resides there...

that allow all the deep

sub-conscious/unconscious change

you desire...

to be made real

in just the right way

for you...

'1 SLEEP!'

You are there and here...

here and now...

in just the right place...

for deep hypnosis,

deep trance,

learning in hypnotic sleep

without effort...

a place where these words,

these ideas can become

your beliefs

and your beliefs become your thoughts now...

the very deepest levels of hypnosis

and trance

that you can experience,

NOOOOOW!'

(Throw in a 'That's right!' if you feel so inclined.)

Again you have done well young Padawan: soon the hypnotic mastery you desire will be yours!

The Rogue hypnotist signing off…for now…

Printed in Great Britain
by Amazon